scarborough
realists
now

a reprint of the 2008 scarborough exhibition catalogue
with a new introduction by Michael Paraskos

david finnigan
clive head
michael paraskos
nathan walsh
steve whitehead

The **Orage** Press

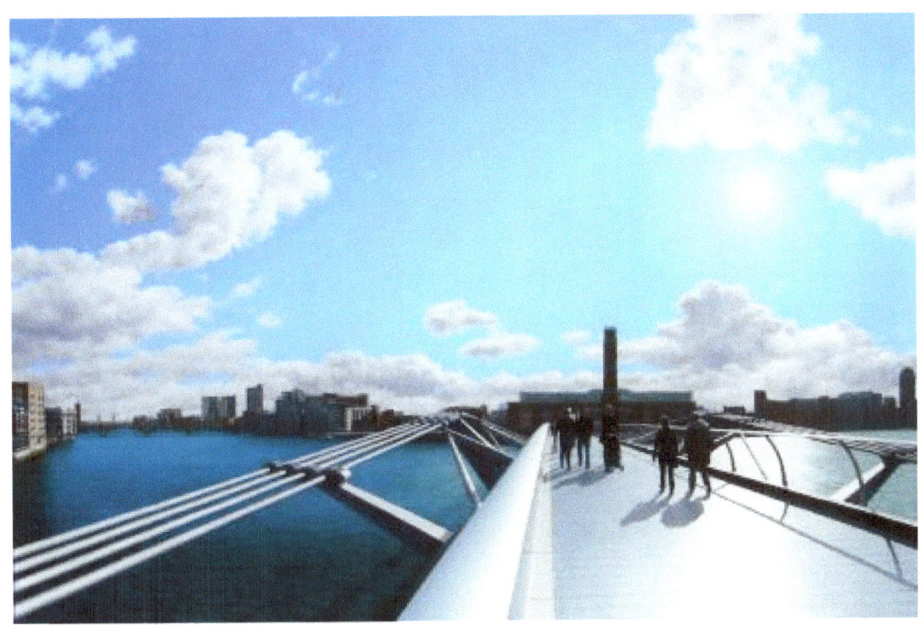

Steve Whitehead
Millennium Bridge, London
Acrylic on canvas 48x72 inches
2008

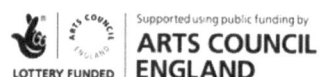

ISBN 978-0-9565802-4-5

Revised second edition with new introduction by Michael Paraskos © 2013 Orage Press.

Clive Head's images appear courtesy of Marlborough Fine Art, London.

Original edition published to accompany the exhibition 'Scarborough Realists Now' held at Scarborough Art Gallery, Scarborough, England, from 4 October to 14 December 2008.

Published in 2013 England (EU) by the Orage Press
16a Heaton Road, Mitcham, Surrey CR4 2BU, England
Printed by Lightningsource

scarborough realists now

The **Orage** Press

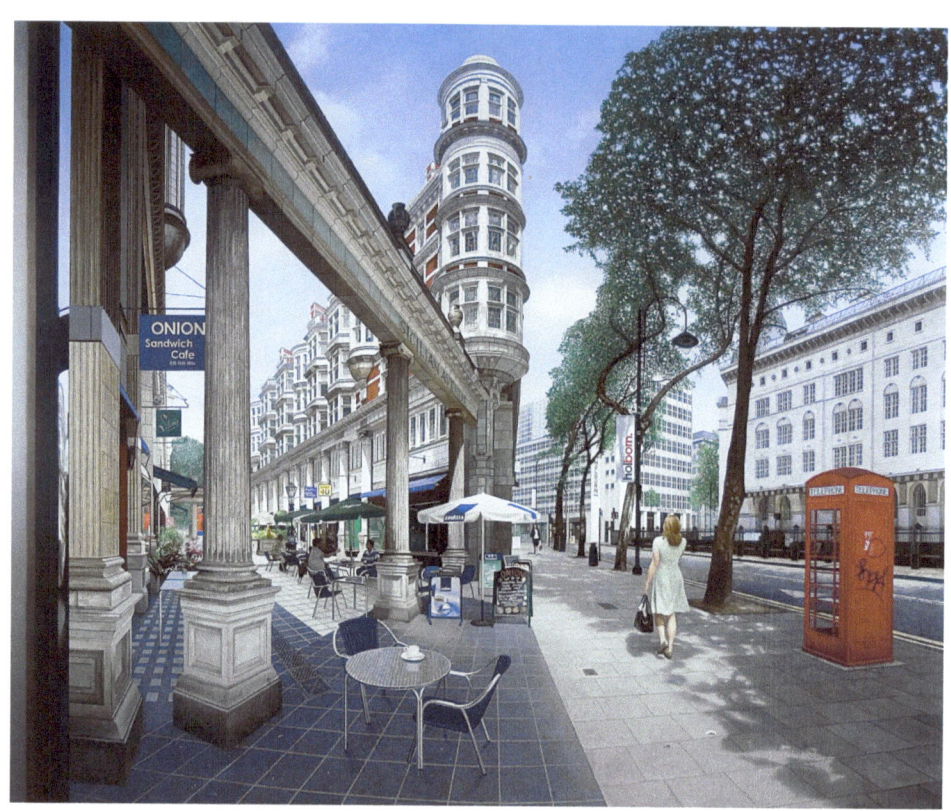

Nathan Walsh
Sicillian Avenue
Oil on canvas 70x84 inches
2007

Beyond Realism Now

a new introduction
by Michael Paraskos

There is something prophetic in the opening line of my original introduction to this catalogue. 'As little as five years ago,' I wrote in 2008, 'it was a particularly difficult life to be an artist who painted realist paintings.'

That was an opening which suggested a change had occurred in the art world in the five years prior to 2008. Undoubtedly that was true, as at least by 2008 fewer serious commentators or artists were rehashing the claim that painting is dead. Something was changing and this exhibition was part of it.

Now, in 2013, a mere five years further on, it is clear attitudes have changed more dramatically than we imagined. Painting has become fashionable again, even finding a home at über-trendy galleries pandering to the whims of tasteless millionaires. Most of that painting might not be very good, a legacy of poor teaching in art schools over the past three or four decades as much as the lack of judgement of wealthy patrons.

But there is a lot of painting about now. And most of that painting is realist, and a great deal of that is Photorealist.

Only five years ago, staging an exhibition of realist painters at a small regional art gallery, well away from the mainstream London or New York art worlds, seemed radical. It was as though we were cocking a snook at the Establishment, dominated as it still was by vacuous post-conceptualism. I don't think such an exhibition would really seem radical now. In fact realist painting, particularly Photorealist painting, has become so ubiquitous it is itself part of the mainstream. There are galleries specialising in it, not only in New York but in places like London and Amsterdam.

So mainstream is Photorealism now that it warranted a major show at the Guggenheim in Berlin in 2009, followed a year later by another at the modish Kunsthal in Rotterdam. While the Berlin exhibition concentrated on the original Photorealists of the late 1960s and early 1970s, the Rotterdam show brought the story up to date by including contemporary realists and Photorealists.

These were not one off events. In Madrid in the Spring of 2013 another survey of Photorealist painting was staged at the Thyssen-Bornemisza Museum, and that show travelled to Birmingham City Art Gallery in the UK in the Autumn of 2013. For many years now, if you have visited almost any contemporary art fair you will have seen Photorealists. One of them, the British artist Mustafa Hulusi, has even been selected for the Venice Biennale, while another, George Shaw, managed to get nominated for the Tate Gallery's Turner Prize in 2011.

That might all suggest a cause for celebration. The foolish cry 'painting is dead' is long since consigned to the dustbin of history, and the painting that seems to be coming to dominate in our age is at least realist, and often photographically realist. Even loose brush painters like Elizabeth Peyton are really Photorealists, although some tight-arsed Photorealists who try to use paint to emulate the dull and undifferentiated surface of a photograph might disagree with that assessment. But the point is there is little cause to celebrate. Photorealism might be everywhere, but the vast majority of it is so bad, made by people so ignorant as to what constitutes art, that one is left pining for the awfulness of the conceptualist art world that preceded it. Who would have imagined that!

I do not think I am alone in nostalgia for the days when followers of a wife-assaulting pillar of the Establishment like Charles Saatchi ruled the art world. Far from being a victory, the triumph for paint now is not a triumph for painting: it is a triumph for image making in paint, with very few of the New Generation Photorealists able to tell the difference between a painting and an image. In this they resemble the very same conceptualist

artists they often claim to despise, and
who they have in part displaced. Like those
conceptualists most of the New Generation
Photorealists are still the heirs to Andy
Warhol, and not genuine artists. To put it
simply their painted images are always trapped in
our world. They reflect our world. In the case of a
conceptualist the art object reflects an idea or
concept in our world. In the case of a New
Generation Photorealist it reflects a
representation or photograph of our world.
For both the art object is no more than a
signifier of an existing reality. True art, true
painting, on the other hand, always creates
its own reality. It is never trapped by our
everyday mundane reality. It is a creative
act and in that act of creation it leaves
existing reality behind to establish
something new, a whole new reality that
has never existed before. That reality might
look a bit like our own reality, and so we might
call the painting 'realist'. But the same
basic principle that underpins this creation
of an alternative 'realist' reality also

underpins the creation of an alternative abstract reality because in true art both the realist and the abstractionist try to step outside of the known mundane reality of everyday existence to create a new credible alternative existence. That is what art is.

This is simple to describe of course, but not simple to do. The problem we face with the vast majority of New Generation Photorealist painters is that very few of them even realise this is the function of art, the reason to make a painting in the first place. So they do not even try to do it. Amongst the New Generation Photorealists there is no philosophical rejection of the definition of art I have given here, there is bafflement and ignorance. It is difficult to conceive of an artist who is ignorant of art. At best it shows what Jean-Paul Sartre called 'bad faith' amongst the New Generation Photorealists, but at worst it leads one to conclude that the vast majority of New Generation Photorealist painters are not artists, and so there is little to celebrate in their rise. They are the Tea Party in paint.

I do not think in 2008 I was quite so scathing of the emergent New Generation Photorealists, but the basic message was undoubtedly there. Rereading the original introduction and essays on the artists it is clear I was already skeptical of the legitimacy of the painter turning him or herself into a human photocopier, something that would no doubt also be confirmed by the newspaper reviews I was writing at the time. What I find intriguing is the consistency of my own belief in the artist as the creator of new worlds. I had thought this had come later from looking at Greek Orthodox religious paintings, in which the painter is believed by the faithful to open up windows into Heaven. But it is here. Later though, I did couple it with a growing interest in anarchist art theory. There was a real logic in doing so which was not mentioned in the original 2008 publication, but which became apparent to me later on.

The anarchists' rejection of existing society is not, in philosophical terms, because they want chaos to reign. It is so space can be opened up to allow a new world, a new reality we might say, to be revealed. In other words, it is to allow us to see a kind of 'heaven'. In art there is the same rejection of existing reality. The function of art requires the rejection of existing notions of time, space, narrative, form and all the other things that define our reality so as to allow a new reality to be opened up on (or should that be in) the canvas. But rather than coming to me from Greek Orthodox aesthetic theory or anarchist art theory and then being applied to contemporary art I realise now that it has in part come from looking at paintings like those in this catalogue. It is almost ironic that looking at realist paintings has led me to an understanding of art that is truly hyper-realist in the sense that hyper means to transcend, to transcend reality, not to iterate it.

What made this exhibition remarkable
was not that it was a showcase of Photorealist
painters exhibiting in a mainstream art world
that seemed to despise both painters and
Photorealism. What made it remarkable was
that it was not a show of Photorealist painters.
If the word hyper-realism had not been
misappropriated by some of the
photocopying realists one might call the
four artists who exhibited in Scarborough
'hyper-realist', not because of their realism,
their use of photography or their paint
surfaces, but because they each sought in
their own way to transcend existing reality
(the 'hyper' of 'hyper-realism') and create
alternative realities of art. In this they were
each the philosophical heirs to Coleridge
and Schelling, Worringer and Fichte, with
more in common with the champion of
abstract art Herbert Read than a long term
champion of Photorealism like Louis Meisel.

Had we recognised this consciously at
the time I think we might have made more
of it. It is here by implication in the
essays, to which none of the four

artists objected, but instead of Scarborough Realists Now perhaps we should have been more prescient and called the show 'Beyond Realism'. That is easy to say in retrospect, of course, but five years ago things seemed very different. Nonetheless it is a fact that has been more than confirmed by the subsequent direction taken by these artists in their art. They have each moved beyond realism, to the point where it is difficult to talk of them now being realists at all, and impossible to define any of them as Photorealists. They are all the better for it.

In some ways this makes this catalogue an historic document, recording a moment in time when a radical art agenda was formed outside the mainstream and then moved centre stage. In a sense that was literal for these artists as they have each become exhibitors in the international art world, but it is also a question of an idea moving from the periphery to the centre. That is how radical change always happens in the art world. It starts in an obscure location and eventually is taken up by the mainstream. It never starts in the centre. The sad thing is that it was a misunderstood version of this radical art agenda that moved centre stage. Ignorant owners of private galleries specialising in realist art in London have pushed an emasculated version of the agenda, simplifying it down to their own level, and rendering it dull and worthless. In that form New Generation Photorealism has been easily taken up by every amateur painter able to hold a pencil the right way up and trace a projected image.

Paradoxically it is the ubiquity of the human photocopiers that reveals just how special this exhibition was, how significant this catalogue is, and how important to the future of painting these artists have become. In 2008 our exhibition in Scarborough was an act of resistance against the dominance of conceptualism. It clearly struck a chord as so many realists and Photorealists emerged subsequently from the woodwork. Some had been working quietly for years, but without a public platform. Others were new to painting. The problem is so many of them have remained wedded to a simple realist and Photorealist agenda, becoming a parody of the radical approach seen in the artists in this show in 2008. They have remained identikit realist painters and as such their conservative and repetitive method offers an extreme contrast to the sheer talent and vision of the artists who came together in a small seaside town in the north of England for this exhibition. While the followers have remained static, reproducing the same formula again and again, each of the four artists who showed in Scarborough has moved on, revolutionising their own artistic agendas in increasingly unique and individual ways. It is a curious paradox that those painters who fail to do this, who just stick to the tired and tested Photorealist formulæ, only succeed in revealing that these four artists and the intellectual underpinning of this show is still extraordinary and significant.

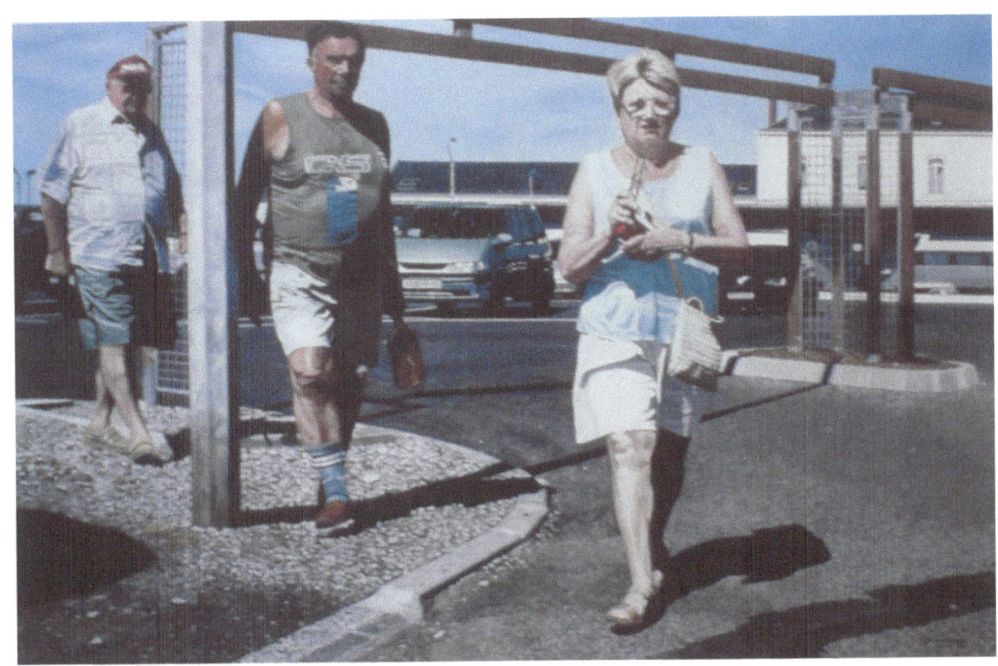

David Finnigan
Evolution
Oil on canvas 30x42 inches
2002

A New Realism

Original introduction
to the 2008 catalogue
by Michael Paraskos

As little as five years ago it was a particularly difficult life to be an artist who painted realist paintings. That is not to say it is now easy to make, exhibit and earn a living from this work, but there has at least been a move in the art world away from dismissing realist painting out-of-hand, towards accepting it as part of a revitalisation of art in England. As a consequence, realist paintings of varying types and quality can now be seen even at fashionable art venues, including the Hayward Gallery, Tate Britain, the BP Portrait Prize, the Jerwood Painting Prize and the John Moores Biennial.

There is no doubt that Scarborough has played a particularly important role in this shift. It has been a location where new realist ideas and practices have had the space to develop and grow away from the often hostile glare of England's mainstream art world. History shows that such a distance from the mainstream centres is often necessary for the development of new ideas in art, and it is only after that initial development has taken place that the new ideas can start to enter the mainstream art world and take over. Of course, it is premature to say whether realist painting is now taking over mainstream English art, but the increasing prevalence of photo-based painting in the mainstream art world does suggest a move in that direction. The increasingly ubiquitous presence of the Photorealist painter Jason Brooks in the trendy end of that art world also suggests a move towards realism, and Brooks is another English realist painter who owes a great debt to Scarborough, where he taught alongside Clive Head, Steve Whitehead and myself in the 1990s.

The shift of interest I am describing here is palpable, but not complete, and we can say without any fear of serious contradiction that we are still in the middle of a process that could lead almost anywhere. We are clearly moving away from the conceptualist art world that dominated in England at the end of the last century, but it is too early to say what we are moving toward. Certainly there are trends that seem to have some significance. For example, student surveys and newspaper articles in recent years have shown a profound dissatisfaction amongst many art students in English art schools at the failure of their tutors to teach them real technical skills, such as paint handling, colour theory and life drawing. This could transform into a significant art movement, and possibly a realist art movement with an understanding of how to handle paint, control colour and draw being important elements in realism. Similarly realist painting could benefit from the fact that the media has also shown itself to be increasingly tired old conceptualist art events such as the Turner Prize, resulting in a dramatic reduction in press coverage. However trends are not outcomes, and it is possible a wholly new attitude to art will emerge that no one saw coming, just as Modernism seemed, to many people, to spring from nowhere in England in 1910. So, perhaps, 2010 is when it really all changes.

If realist painting is to be an element in the new art that is emerging then the paintings of David Finnigan, Clive Head, Nathan Walsh and Steve Whitehead offer a good starting point to see the differences in approach that realist artists can employ. In effect there is no such thing as realism, there are realisms (note the plural), and the overlaps between different realist artists might not be as significant as their differences. For example, although all four of these artists use photography as a tool in their work, they do not do so in the same way. This is evident from the look of their paintings, but it is also in the background, in their approaches and technical processes to making their works. It ranges from Finnigan's emphasis on getting the initial photograph as 'right' as possible, so that it provides what he calls a 'good foundation' for the painted image, to Head's far more composite approach, which brings together dozens of separate images, not all of which are photographic.

One of the most likely responses to these paintings is that they 'look real', and certainly that is an element of this kind of realism. Not all realisms do this, so it is a specific aesthetic that is very different to the art of, say, the Impressionists or the Pre-Raphaelites, who were also realists. Yet, I think it is also worth approaching these artists' paintings with the deliberate aim of thinking they do not look real. No painting that deserves the name of art ever seeks to simply reproduce reality as that would be a futile exercise. There is no point in reproducing something that already exists as we can simply go and look at the real thing itself. So art always sets itself the goal of creating something that is different to reality, even if that art is, in some sense, realistic.

In some cases this difference to our reality can be pointed out quite easily. Whitehead's images, for example, are often strangely still, far more so than the location he paints would be in real life, and, even when he paints city streets, he orders the elements of the city far more than they would be in real life. The chaotic crowds of people who throng our cities are reduced in number, or discarded altogether, as though Whitehead is trying to visualise an ideal version of these places.

Yet the most obvious difference to reality can be seen in all of these artists' work, and that is the fact that the worlds they create are out of reach of the viewer. We can see those worlds, as though these paintings are windows, but, unlike a window, we cannot unlock the catch, open the pane and jump into the scene. It exists on the other side of an invisible barrier that prevents us from physically entering the painted space, a barrier that is called the picture plane. This is not to say we are permanently excluded from the image, but we have to use different human faculties to enter it. So, because we cannot actually walk into one of Whitehead's landscapes or Walsh's cityscapes, we have to engage in an act of imagining ourselves into the picture. This act of imagination goes under many different names, but one of the most useful is the term 'empathy'. By empathising with the illusion of space in the picture we are able to imagine ourselves into the picture, and in this way all the painters' works we see in this exhibition cease to be illusions of reality, and become instead alternative realities.

This aspect of painting is not unique to realist painting. Indeed it underpinned the beliefs of the abstract painter Wassily Kandinsky at the beginning of the last century, and without it a justification for any form of painting as an art form is difficult to make. As human beings we need psychological spaces in which alternative versions of reality can either offer a counterbalance to our actual existence, or a potential new existence to which we can strive. Perhaps one of Whitehead's ideal landscapes, in which chaos is banished, is a necessary psychological balance to the chaos in our everyday lives, as though the world on this side of the picture plane is evened out by the world he has created on the other side of the picture plane. Similarly, perhaps the calm and order of one of Finnigan's still lives is a necessary balance to the lack of calm and order in our lives. I admit this is a radical deviation from the mainstream view that art reflects society, but I go back to a point I made earlier –if art is merely going to reflect life there is no point in having art as we have life.

There is one final point that should be made in relation to this and other forms of realist art being made in England to-day. The best art is always rooted in a specific geographical, environmental and cultural location. The idea of internationalism in art is an unhealthy myth that leads people to turn their work into something so generic it is unpalatably bland. This is not the same as saying art is a reflection of society, any more than a tree with roots merely reflects the soil in which it is planted. Nonetheless that tree grows in a particular way because of that soil. Although it is clear these artists have a knowledge and admiration for American forms of realism, and particularly Photorealism, it needs to be remembered that realism has a long history in the Germanic part of Europe, stretching from Germany itself, through Scandinavia and the Low Countries, and into England. It is one of the most dominant forms of art in the history of these regions. In the best works by these artists I think we can see that history as a living thing, influenced by American and other artists, but also drawing on the traditions of northern European, and specifically English, realism. There is no doubt these are contemporary paintings, but lessons from artists such as

Constable and Turner, and groups such as the Norwich School and Camden Town artists, are also there if you give the paintings time and consideration to see them.

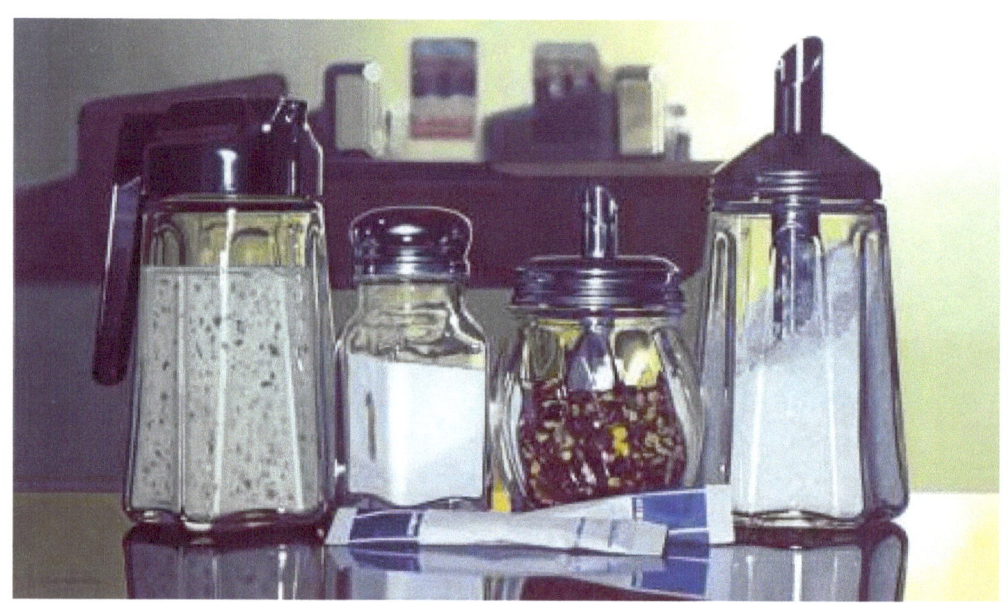

David Finnigan
Here and Now
Oil on linen 30x42 inches
2002c

David Finnigan

The work of David Finnigan is perhaps the closest of the four artists to an historic photorealist method, although like his colleagues, Finnigan shuns the label 'photorealism'. Instead he prefers to call his work Contemporary Realism. In this he may be right. Finnigan might have a working method that resembles that of the early American Photorealists, but he differs from them in several key ways. Before we look at some of the differences, however, it is useful to think about how Finnigan's work draws on the tradition of American Photorealism.

Like many of the American Photorealists, the primary transformation of any subject that Finnigan paints, such as a cityscape, still life or shop window, takes place within the camera, long before any brush has touched a canvas, or perhaps even any canvas has been stretched on to a frame. This means the actuality of life, with its ordinariness and chaos, has to become extraordinary and ordered at the moment when the camera shutter is clicked, rather than through any later manipulation of the photographic image as it is transferred into paint. As Finnigan states, when taking the photograph, the artist chooses 'the subject matter, its brightness range, the colours involved, the point of focus and the extent of the depth of field'. If the artist gets these right, he says, they 'provide the foundation of the painting'.

As with many of the American Photorealists, however, this raises the serious question as to the purpose of the painting if all the creative decisions have already been taken prior to its creation. There is a very real danger that the artist will become no more than a photographic enlarging machine, who might take a well-crafted, or even artistic, photograph, but do no more in paint than blow the image up with a high degree of verity to the original photographic source. Indeed, this is often the criticism, and the misguided praise,

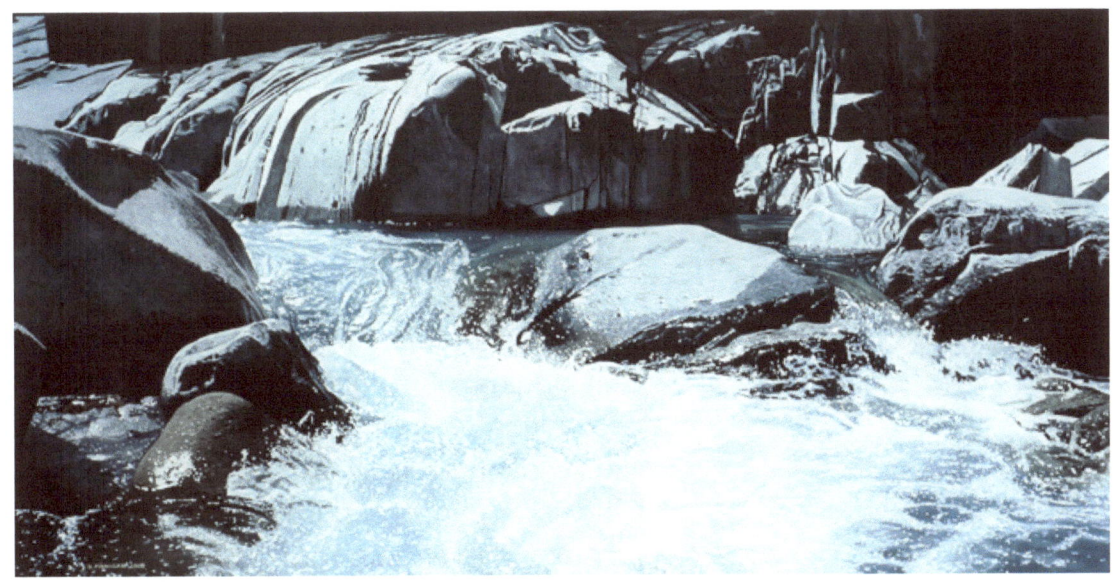

David Finnigan
Reuss
Oil on canvas 48x66 inches
2008

heaped on photo-based realist art, that the act of making the painting is rendered redundant by the predetermined nature of the final image. If a photograph is turned into a painting, even with a high level of faithfulness to the original photograph, then we might well argue that the art lies in that original photograph and not in the subsequent painting. In a sense it is rather like reversing the old question as to whether a photographic reproduction of a painting is ever as good as the original. Only a semiotician is likely to argue that the photograph of a painting by, say, Constable or Turner is as good as the original, and so in Finnigan's work we are entitled to ask whether the reproduction of an original photograph in paint is ever as good as the original photograph.

Although many contemporary Photorealist painters seem unaware of this issue, Finnigan knows very well the implications of his working method, and like the other three artists in this exhibition, takes measures to counteract any problem with it. In his case these measures are essential to understanding how his work differs from standard Photorealism.

Finnigan is very clear that when he uses a photograph in his work he is not a machine enlarging a photograph, rather he is a human being. From that simple fact he is able to acknowledge that human vagaries do creep into the work. A machine might make a perfect copy of a perfect line in a photograph, but a human being cannot, even if the immediate impression for a viewer, when they look at that line, is that it is perfect. Subtly, and almost imperceptibly, Finnigan's work will possess a human, and not a mechanical, characteristic. Equally important is the fact that Finnigan acknowledges that he is using paint to make his paintings, and unlike some other contemporary Photorealists, does not try to hide this fact. Again, this might seem a simple thing to state, but by acknowledging that the medium of paint is intrinsically different to the medium of photography Finnigan seeks to avoid the fundamental mistake, so many other current Photorealists make, of trying to make paintings that look like photographs. And there is no doubt that, for all their photograph-like quality, Finnigan's paintings do not look like blown-up photographs. In them there is an acknowledgement of what used to be called the 'painterliness' of paint.

Of course we are not talking about the level of painterliness we see in a Claude Monet or a Jackson Pollock, but there is a celebration of paint as a medium that links Finnigan's work to that of more loose-brush painters. The result of this is that we are never in any doubt we are looking at paintings based on photographs, and not simple-minded painted photographs.

This can be seen very clearly in a work such as Evolution (2002), in which any minute detailing is counterposed against areas in which there is a broadening out of the brushwork. One can compare the level of finish on the green car in the middle distance, for example, with that of the skin of the woman in the foreground, to see a range of different techniques in the application of paint, all of which indicates a desire to avoid simply reproducing a photograph. The debt of honour here is to Ralph Goings, one of the leading first generation American Photorealists, and in whose scenes of figures, cars and American diners there is a similar interest in the almost abstract quality of paint, as much as in the ability to emulate a photograph. This is a little-recognised aspect of first-generation Photorealism that a small number of the new realists have taken on board, and it has allowed them to use photography as a tool whilst avoiding the dead end of copying photographs.

In Finnigan an admiration for Goings can also be seen in a number of still life images he has produced, such as Here and Now. In these Finnigan seems to emulate Going's signature-piece images of tableware in American diners, in which depictions of ketchup bottles, sugar jars and salt and pepper pots take centre stage. Yet, what seems to happen in Finnigan's work is that there is a simplification of the elements. As viewers we are generally much closer to the objects than we would be in a Goings, and the backgrounds are more abstract, all of which suggests these paintings are intended to say less about the specific places in which they are set than about the abstract relationships between each of the objects shown. Goings does this too, of course. but whereas a Goings still life is undeniably an American table setting in an American diner, Finnigan does not give us an English cafe as an equivalent. Rather, he seems to be aiming for an image that is less geographically specific, and in a way more rarefied, or, at least, that is the type of image he achieves. In Here and Now we can see a glass, a polished steel sugar pot.

a milk jug and a salt cellar on a highly polished table-top.

That level of shine, and the sheer cleanliness of the objects themselves, indicates a desire to perfect our world rather than evoke an actual English greasy spoon cafe in a northern English seaside town. Although the evocation of a specific time and place is an important element in art, there is also room for those who would perfect the world. It would not surprise me, after looking at these paintings, if that is the direction in which Finnigan's future lies.

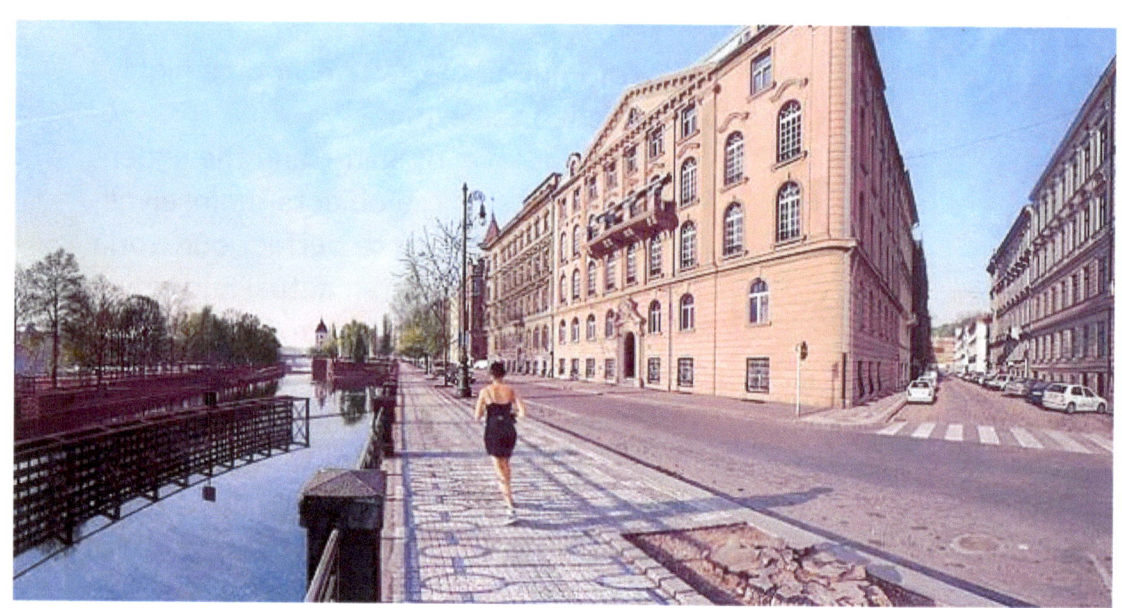

Clive Head
Prague, Early Morning
Oil on canvas 52x98 inches
2004-2006

Clive Head

Clive Head is undoubtedly one of the most talented British artists of his generation. This is easily seen in terms of the quality of his work, but it is also apparent in the originality of his ambition. Yet that ambition might come as a surprise to many people, as Head's stated aim is to rework an art movement that few people are likely to associate him with. Head seeks nothing less dramatic than refraire le cubism sur nature.

Cubism was, of course, the art form developed by Georges Braque and Pablo Picasso in the early years of the twentieth century. As every art history student should know, it involved an image, usually a still life, being apparently shattered; the shattered image was then reassembled in a new form. What was important about this method, however, was that the image was not shattered from a single point of view, but in three dimensions. The result was that the reconstructed image could show you parts of the original objects from different angles, as well as some parts close up and others at a distance. We might look at the front of a wine bottle, but also at its top and base. We might see the front and back of a violin, but its neck might be rendered larger, as though we have picked it up and are examining this part of the instrument more closely. What Cubism attempted to do was shatter not the single point of view of an object, as though cutting up a flat photograph with scissors, but shatter and reassemble the experience of walking around, say, a still life. That experience might lead us to move in closer on part of an object, to focus on one particular thing, and then move out again, to gain a more holistic view.

Of course, looking at a painting by Head, the image does not appear to be shattered, but it is no less a composite image than a cubist painting. Contrary to the assumption many people have when seeing one of Head's paintings, the image is not a painting of a single photograph or a single point of view; rather it is an amalgam of many different photographs –perhaps as many as one hundred per painting. Into this are added freehand drawings the artist has made, all of which which form different points of view. This is most clearly seen, or at least explained, through Head's series of 'coffee shop paintings'. In one of the most recent, Rebekah (2008) we can see a figure in a red dress, apparently sitting in front of us, at a table, in a Nero coffee shop.

At first sight it might appear a simple reproduction of a simple scene –one familiar in almost any town– but the image has been constructed from a myriad of other images. The table was probably derived from two or three individual photographs of a table in the coffee shop. Similarly, the lamps hanging down, the floor and the assorted paraphernalia that distinguish a Nero coffee shop from a Starbucks or a Pret-a-Manger also came from many different photographs. This

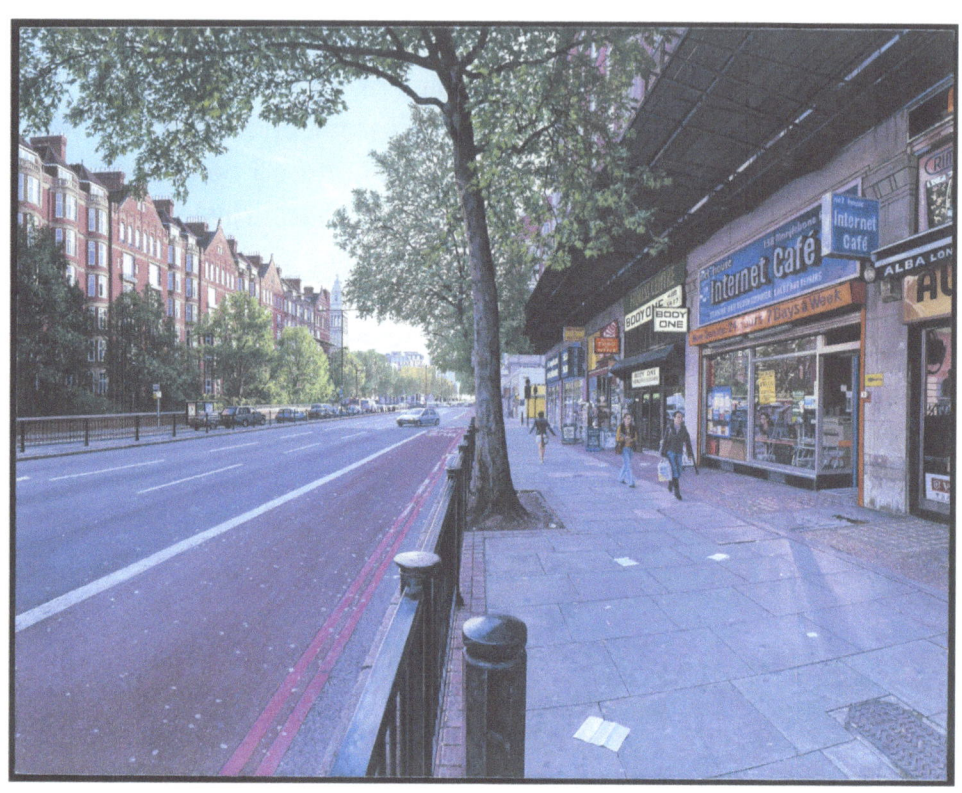

Clive Head
Marylebone Road
Oil on canvas 45x52 inches
2006

means we are not looking at the reproduction of a photograph that has been taken and then painted. Rather, the image is fabricated from many different images. It would be more accurate to say it is fabricated from many different sources of information as the figure in the painting was not derived from a photograph at all, but drawn from life, and whereas the coffee shop is located in London's Piccadilly, the model sat for Head in his studio in Scarborough.

Once we have established that Head's painting is not the reproduction of a photograph. or even a composite of several photographs, we can start to see that the space in the painting is rather curious. If we look out of the window, the space in the street is clearly treated in a different way to the interior space near the woman in red. The outside and the interior space obey different rules so that the lines of perspective, the question of scale and our orientation are not the same throughout the painting. Look to the left of the figure and the interior of the coffee shop also seems to obey different spatial rules, almost as though we are looking at one of those cubist paintings of a bottle or violin, or even a human figure, and seeing some of the shattered image close-up, other parts far away and others up-ended.

Where Head differs from Braque or Picasso, of course, is that he creates a pictorial space in which these shifts of perspective do not jar, even though they are, if anything, even more extreme than anything attempted by the cubists. We can see that extremity when we look at a painting such as Prague, Early Morning (2004-2006). Again, this is not a painting reproducing a single photograph of a single view, but a composite of many photographs, some of which concentrate on small details, others on the vistas. In this painting the view down the street has to coexist with a simultaneous view down the river, and another view across the river.

Yet to our right is a street running at almost 90 degrees to the river. which means our total field of view runs around, perhaps, 180 degrees, or even nearer 210 degrees.

One's initial reaction to this is that Head creates images that show us more than we could possibly see if we stood, say, on the nominative spot for this painting –that is on the riverside in Prague –because no forward facing human eye can take in at one glance 210 degrees of a scene. This achievement is clearly masterful in terms of technique, but it also runs the risk of dehumanising the artwork because it removes the artwork from actual human experience. Of course, a great deal of photo-based realism is dehumanised for this very reason, with painters subsuming their humanity into the mechanics of a Photoshop computer graphics program. As we have already seen with Head's working technique, however, he is not really interested in going over the increasingly tired ground of using paint to

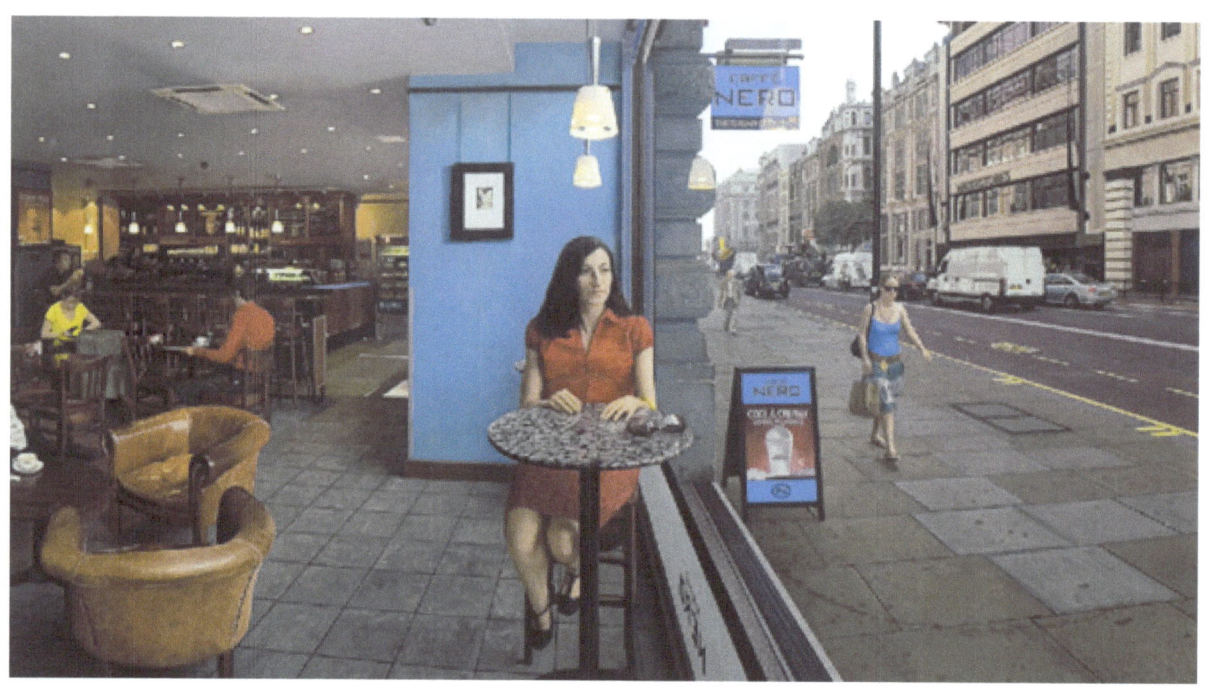

Clive Head
Rebekah
Oil on canvas 65x85 inches
2008

question the nature of photography. Instead he wants to use paint to make paintings that explore humanity, one of the most ancient reasons for picking up a paint brush in the first place. That is also one of the reasons he introduces pencil drawing into his toolbox, with pencil drawing, particularly from the live model, being one of the most intimate, and therefore human, processes of art-making.

It is out of this that a paradoxical truth emerges, whereby Head shows us scenes that are more than the eye can see, but which also mimic the way we see. We all know that as human beings we do not experience the world in one glance, rather we let our eyes dart around a scene. Our heads and bodies move, panning along a river or a street, and we might focus on one thing, then another and then take in the whole view. In other words, there is nothing mechanistic in the way Head extends the visual field in his paintings, rather there is an acknowledgement that to be human is not to passively take in a scene, but to actively seek out elements within a location that are of interest to us. These elements of interest form pockets of space on which we focus, and with our eyes and brain we treat each pocket of space as a distinct entity.

Thus, if we are in a coffee shop, we might focus for a moment on the face of the woman in the red dress, but then we look down at our coffee cup. We might look out of the window, up the street and across it, and then back into coffee shop, at the bar, the fridge, the lights and the other customers. Each of these views would form a pocket of space, and on each space our brains refocus the eyes, editing out unnecessary detail and re-aligning our binocular sight. As this happens, however, we are not shocked by a fragmented set of different visual experiences, as though this is shattered sight akin to a cubist painting. On the contrary, it appears to us to be a

continuous experience, not unlike the
coherent worlds created by Head.

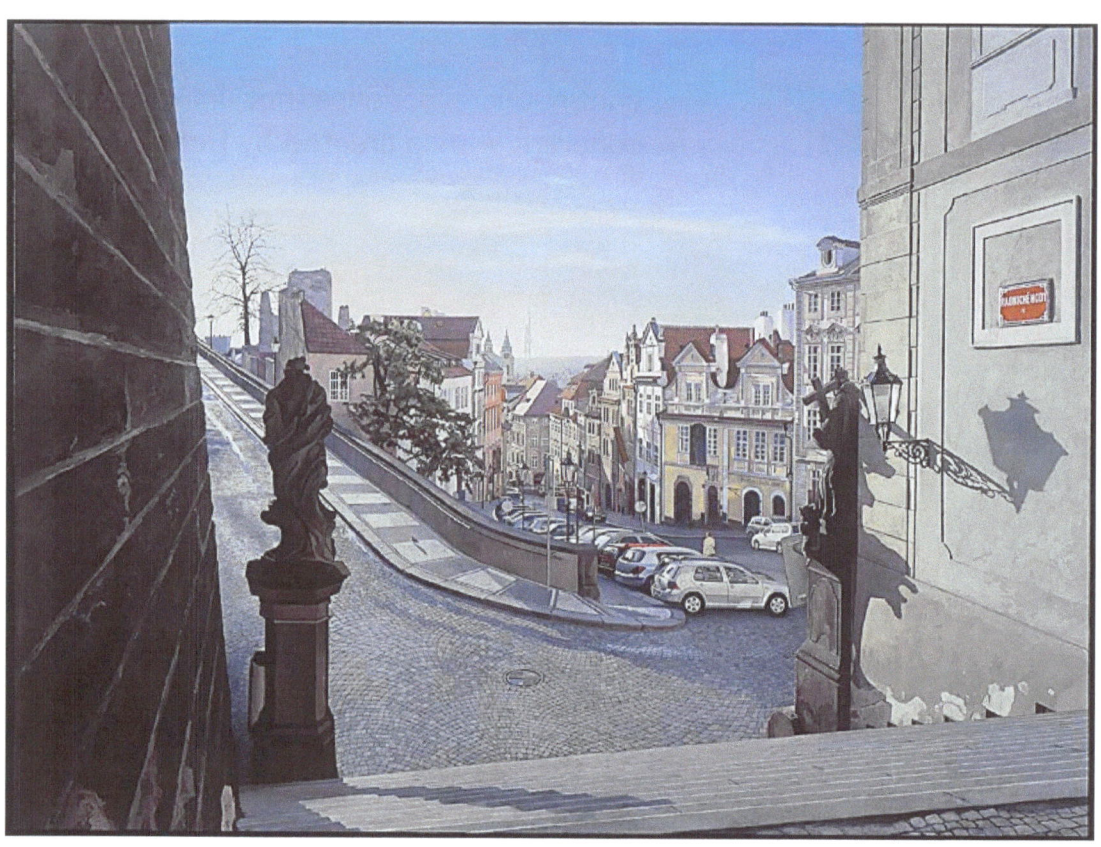

Nathan Walsh
Prague, Morning Sun
Oil on canvas 51x68 inches
2007

Nathan Walsh

Nathan Walsh is the youngest of the four painters here, and although he is an accomplished and experienced artist. there is no doubt his work is evolving.

In a painting such as Prague Morning Sun (2007) Walsh has used a composite method, in which several elements, including more than one photograph, sketches and, importantly, a knowledge of art history, have been brought together to create the image. In this Walsh owes something of a debt to Clive Head, and as in Head's work what is achieved by Walsh is not a reproduction of what one would have seen had one stood next to him as he began taking his photographs on that sunny morning in Prague in 2007. Rather it is a fantasised view, in which a whole range of different elements have been brought together, and filtered through the artist's mind, to become what seems like a coherent whole.

Calling any form of realism fantasy is, of course, counter-intuitive, but realism does share a curious relationship with fantasy art. The type of image we see on the covers of science fiction novels, by fantasy artists such as Stephan Martiniere, might show imagined alien worlds thousands of light years away, but the techniques Martinere and his colleagues use are often very similar to realism, and particularly Photorealism. This is evident not only in the hyper 'realistic' detail shown, but in the way images are composed and the viewpoint of the imagined spectator. These realist-derived techniques are used precisely because fantasy artists want to persuade their viewers to suspend their disbelief and accept the scene is somehow real. Although he is firmly earthbound, Walsh's images are no more real than those of the fantasy artist, but his fantasy is a Prague street on a pretty morning, or the view of a strangely named sandwich shop, and graffitied telephone box, in London's Holborn.

A sense of the artifice of realism can be gleaned particularly well from a recognition that Walsh is also not simply drawing his source material from the particular places he paints. He is selecting scenes, organising space and orchestrating the action with a knowledge of earlier art in mind. Indeed, like most good realist artists working in Europe today, Walsh is not only indebted to the American Photorealists, but draws influence from earlier European painters of land and cityscapes. This includes obvious names, such as Canaletto, who has had a slightly excessive influence on many contemporary realist artists in both Europe and North America, but also surprising figures such as the early nineteenth-century English artist Richard Parkes Bonington. What we see when we look at one of Walsh's images is not, therefore, a reflection of a particular place, as though the artist holds up a mirror to the world. Such an activity would be futile as we do not need mirrors of a world we can experience directly ourselves.

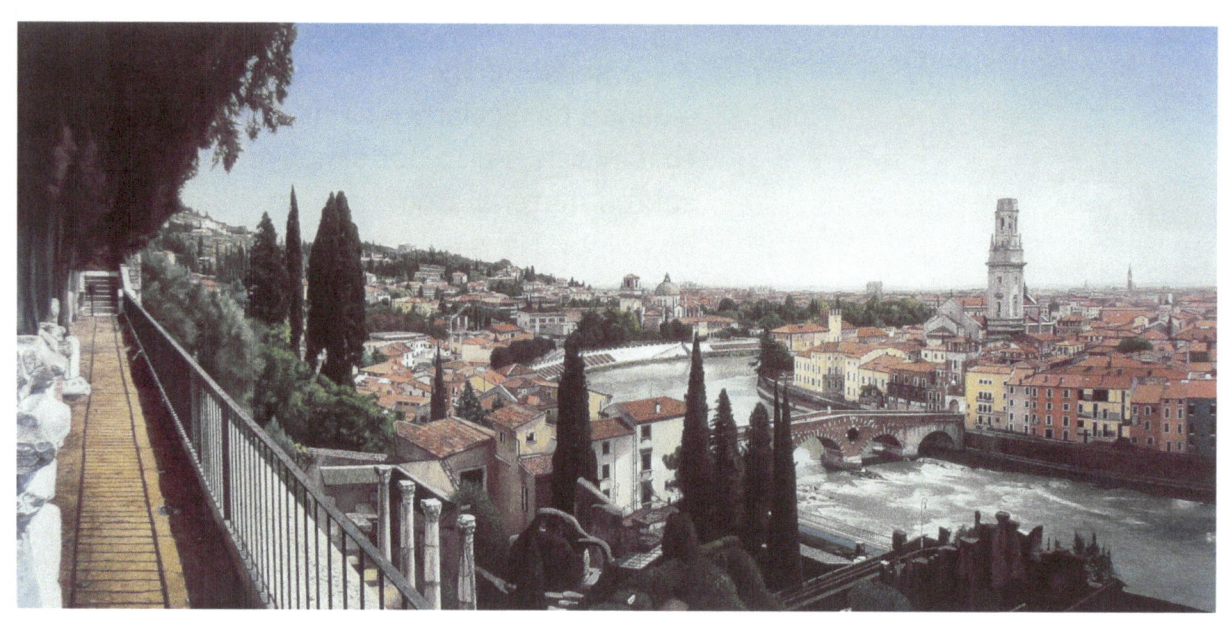

Nathan Walsh
View of Verona from Castell San Pietro
Oil on canvas 34x71 inches
2006

Rather it is a fantasised reality, that exists in a parallel world on the other side of the picture plane that is the surface of the canvas. There is no denying that Walsh's fantasised world includes the experience of particular places, such as Prague, London, Verona, New York and elsewhere, but at its best it is never a single experience of those places. It is always composite, with multiple experiences and a deep experience of the history of art all joining in a complex mix. Yet it is one of the paradoxes of this type of realism that if the artist is successful in combining these different elements into a coherent image the viewer will not necessarily be aware of how artificial the image is. Indeed, most will probably believe they are looking at a straightforward copy of a particular view, or at least a copy of a photograph of a particular view.

As I said at the beginning, Walsh's work is in a process of evolution, a process that should be the hallmark of all good artists. Most notably in his latest works, still in progress in the studio, Walsh seems to be attempting to resolve some of the disparate elements I have mentioned, such as multiple views of a place and a knowledge of the history of art, into a single coherent photograph right at the start. This is a brave move that carries with it a very real risk of failure. As bad Photorealist artists demonstrate, taking a single photograph, projecting it on to a canvas and then copying it exactly in paint, makes for very dull art, even if the original image was stunning. This is because it dehumanises the whole process, turning the painter into no more than a human photocopying machine, when the whole raison d'etre for art is to respond as human beings to the world around us. Walsh is very well aware of this danger, and so mitigates it by still doing a great deal of freehand drawing on the canvas. This shows a recognition that the camera dehumanises the images it creates –it cannot help but do this since it is only an inhuman machine. By drawing freehand, Walsh reinstates the human touch, rehumanising the work and moving his paintings from being an image of Prague or London, to being very specifically Walsh's image of Prague or London.

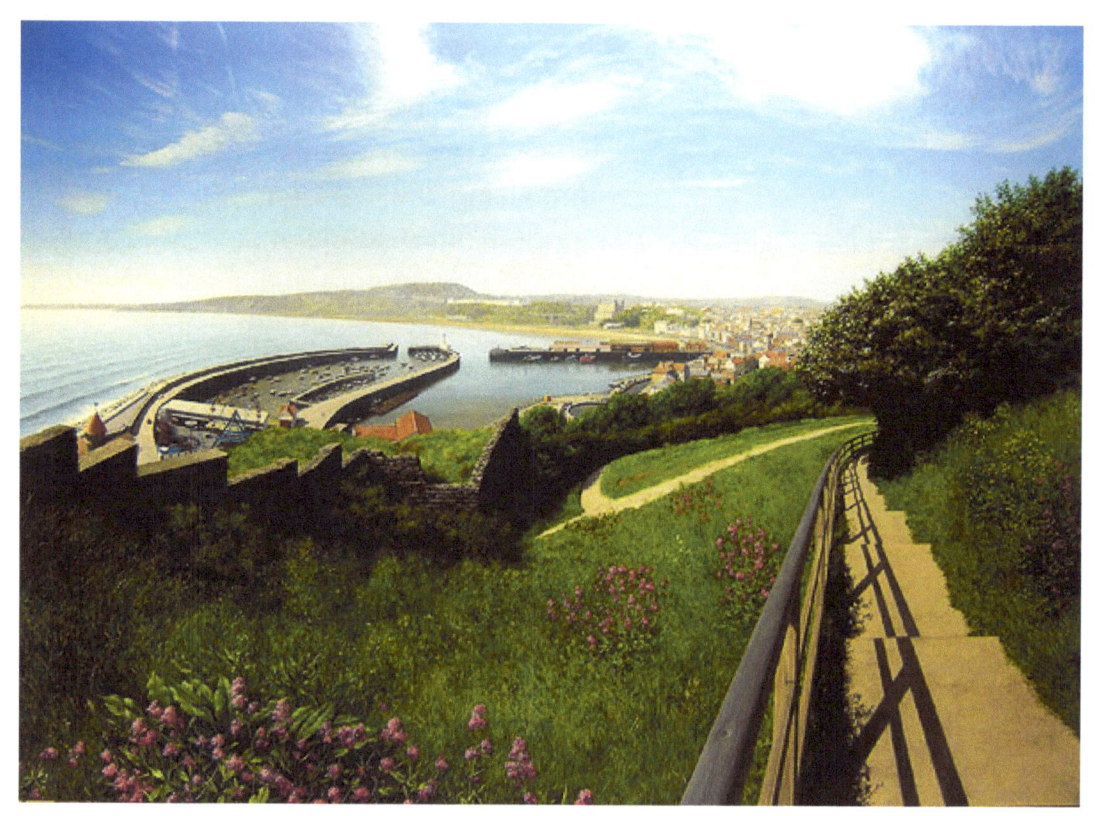

Steve Whitehead
View of Scarborough
Acrylic on canvas 48x66 inches
2005

Steve Whitehead

Realism is a mercurial label that encompasses a huge range of artistic styles, from the Baroque drama of Caravaggio, to the bright paint and loose brushwork of Monet, and the vivid hyper-realism of Chuck Close. Steve Whitehead's art might operate within a realist tradition that is less well-known than these examples, but it is nonetheless one of the most deeply felt and I would say deeply northern forms of realism there is. It has roots in the German Romantic art of Caspar David Friedrich, but also in the quietist traditions of the Danish Biedermeier painters, such as Christian Købke, Johan Thomas Lundbye and Constantin Hansen. Add to this mix Whitehead's interest in English artists such as Edward Wadsworth, Eric Ravilious and Algemon Newton, amongst others, and you have a collection of influences that are coherent, but outside the mainstream.

Curiously, for all these mainland European influences, and the undoubted

61

lessons learned from American Photorealists such as Richard Estes, Whitehead's paintings are also intensely English. To be quite honest, this has only dawned on me very recently, despite knowing the artist and his work for well over a decade. Whilst he shuns the matter-of-fact realism that dominates America, Whitehead also baulks at the willful quirkiness of much contemporary Dutch realism, and offers instead a discreetly eccentric view of the world that is undoubtedly very English. The Englishness that encompasses Whitehead is that of the Avengers, Jonathan Creek, warm beer and cricket, seaside jetties and bright red telephone boxes. It is totally baffling to anyone who is not part of that same English culture, and, like the consummate Englishman he is, Whitehead carries his identity firmly with him, whether he is painting England, Scotland, Italy or Cyprus. This is not a sign of arrogance, or indifference to other cultures. Nor is it an insensitivity to new environments.

It is simply to say that Whitehead, like so many of the best artists, and certainly many of the best English artists, is rooted in a specific time and place. To give it a technical term, it is his egotopography, which the Germans call *Ortgeist*, and his art grows from that *Ortgeist*.

A strong sense of place is certainly evident in a painting such as The Road to Wold Newton (2005). Although there is a very close affinity to Danish landscapes, particularly a work such as Open Country in North Zealand (1842) by Lundbye, Whitehead's painting is undeniably a painting of England by an Englishman. Both Lundbye and Whitehead show similar flat open farmland, and both depict the landscape so that it seems to shoot away from us, with roads and lines of perspective moving across the fields. Both set the viewer at a very low vantage point, allowing space to paint a large expanse of sky. But

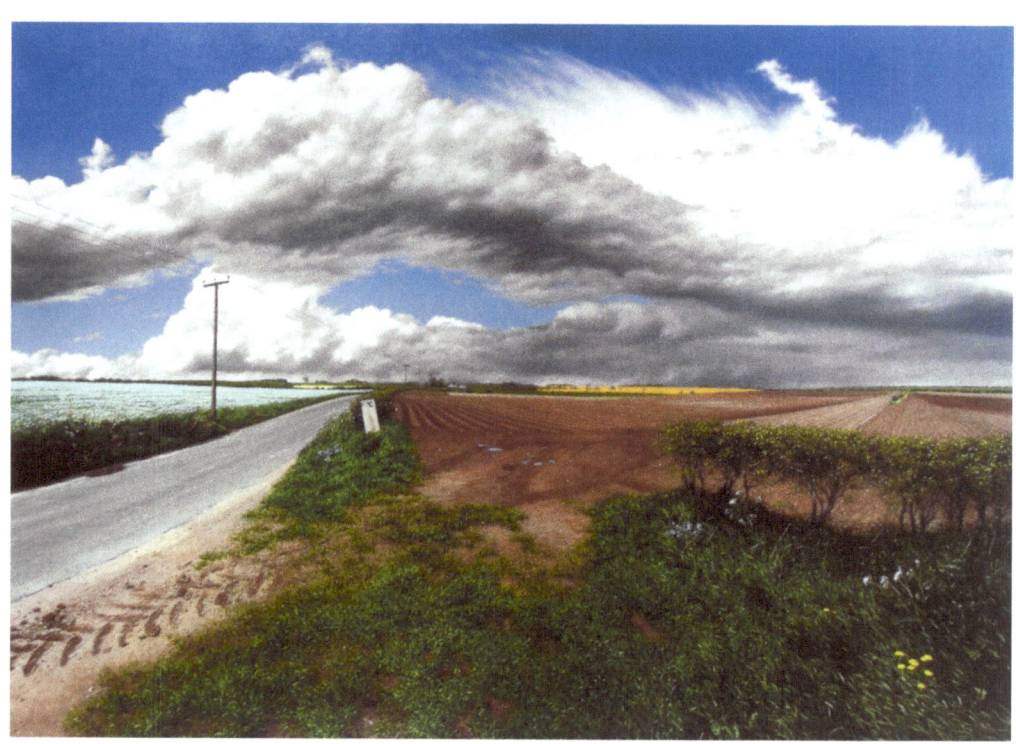

Steve Whitehead
The Road to Wold Newton
Oil on canvas 30x42 inches
2005

it would be difficult to confuse Lundbye's Danish scene for an English view, or Whitehead's image of Yorkshire for anywhere but England. In part this is due to the Englishness of the landscape itself. As anyone who has flown across the North Sea will testify, even the flat landscape of eastern England is very different to the flat landscape of Holland. Those who have crossed the mere 24 miles that are the English Channel will also agree that one of the most striking features of the French farmscape of the Pays de Calais is how un-English it is, and no doubt French travellers crossing the other way note how un-French are the fields of Kent. This is true despite the bedrock beneath those fields, and most of the fauna and flora of the regions, being identical on both sides of the Channel. It indicates very strongly how the land has been shaped not only by Nature, but the hands and minds of the different peoples living on it. The land creates, but also embodies, the egotopographies of its inhabitants.

At an admittedly very simplistic level, one of the most striking differences is the greater sense of rationality and order in the cultivated fields of mainland Europe, whereas here, even in an intensively farmed region such as the Yorkshire wolds, something seems to reflect an English tradition of informal liberty. It is almost as though the cultivated landscape of Europe has been converted to some kind of metric ordering system, whilst those of England remain doggedly. and idiosyncratically. imperial. Like all the best painters of the English landscape, it is this particularity that has been captured by Whitehead. Having said that, Whitehead does not seek simply to reflect reality back to his viewers, and a work like The Road to Wold Newton is not simply a mirror to that part of the world. Whitehead filters the experience of being in this particular place at a particular time through a kind of aesthetic alembic which reconfigures the landscape in ways that are outside nature. In real life it might, for example, be possible to see big, dramatic clouds above Wold Newton, such as those that dominate the sky in Whitehead's painting. But that is to miss the point because the clouds are as much a reflection of a curious tradition of cloud painting in English art, a pastime that occupied many great historic artists such as Gainsborough, Constable and Turner.

Whitehead is not, therefore, just reflecting a part of England as it is, he is creating an alternative world, an artistic world that is based on the aesthetic experience of being a particular person, with a particular history, in a particular place, at a particular time. Within that there is an admiration for historic artists such as Lundbye, and for an English tradition of landscape painting. If Whitehead is successful in distilling these diverse elements into a coherent single image one might not even be aware that this is what he has done. It should look natural –as though it could not possibly look any other way.

Biographies

David Finnigan was born in Fulford near York and studied Fine Art at Falmouth School of Art, gaining a degree there in 1988. Initially his work was influenced by the energy and dynamism of the early twentieth-century art movements of Futurism and Vorticism. A move to a more direct realist style led to him being represented by the London gallery Plus One. His work is now in private and corporate collections nationally and internationally. Recent exhibitions include *Beyond Realism* at Galerie de Bellefeuille, Montreal, Canada in 2012; and *Hyperrealism Today* at the Museo Del Tabac, Andorra in 2013.

Clive Head was born in Maidstone, Kent and educated at the University of Wales, Aberystwyth and Lancaster University. He moved to Scarborough to teach at University College Scarborough where he chaired the Department of Fine Art. In

2010 he staged a solo show at the National Gallery in London, and was included in the exhibition *The Adventure of Reality* at the Kunsthal in Rotterdam in 2011. In 2012 he collaborated with Michael Paraskos in staging a intervention at Dulwich Picture Gallery in London, based on the work of Nicolas Poussin, and in 2013 he was included in the exhibitions *Hyperrealism 1967-2012* at the Thyssen-Bornemisza Museum in Madrid and *Women: Love and Life* at the Lehmbruck Museum in Duisburg, Germany. He has work in collections including Imperial College, London, the Maria Lucia and Ingo Klöcker Collection, the Museum of London and the Victoria and Albert Museum amongst others. Books on Head include *Clive Head Paintings 1996 to 2001* (London: Blains Fine Art, 2001) and *Clive Head: New Paintings* (London: Marlborough, 2007), and *Clive Head* London: Lund Humphries, 2010) written by Michael Paraskos. Head's work is included in *Photorealism at the Millennium* (New York:

Abrams, 2002) and *Photorealism in the Digital Age* (New York: Abrams, 2013) both by Linda Chase and Louis Meisel.

Michael Paraskos was born in Leeds and gained his doctorate, on the art critic Herbert Read, at the University of Nottingham. He has taught at various universities and art colleges in Britain and abroad, was formerly Henry Moore Research Fellow at the University of Leeds, and Research Fellow for Harlow Art Trust. He is Director of the Cyprus College of Art and the Cornaro Institute. He has written extensively on art, education policy and politics for newspapers and magazines, and reviewed exhibitions for BBC Radio 4. He is a book reviewer for several periodicals including *The Spectator*. Book publications include *Steve Whitehead* (London: Orage Press, 2008), *Clive Head* (London: Lund Humphries, 2010) and *Regeneration* (London: Orage Press, 2010). He was editor of the book *Re-Reading Read: New*

Views on Herbert Read (London: Freedom Press, 2007) and has contributed chapters to numerous collaborative books and other publications.

Nathan Walsh was born in Lincoln and completed his MA in Painting at the University of Hull. He has spent the last twelve years dividing his time as a lecturer in art and design and as a practising artist. He has had work exhibited at the Royal Academy, Lambeth Palace and the Mall Galleries. Walsh has exhibited widely around the world including at Metro Gallery, Australia in 2012, the exhibition *Hyper-Realism* at the Albemarle Gallery, London in 2011, KIAF 11 The Korean International Art Fair, Seoul, Korea in 2012, and the Persterer Gallery, Zürich, Switzerland in 2010 amongst others. He has work in public and private collections worldwide.

Steve Whitehead was born in Coventry and was taught painting at the University of

Wales by David Tinker, graduating with an MA in the mid 1980s, before continuing his studies at the Courtauld Institute of Art. He was Head of the MA in Painting programme at the University of Hull's Scarborough Campus, and has taught at various universities and art colleges in Britain and abroad. He has twice won the Wales Open and has also been a prizewinner in Manchester Academy and Hunting Art Prizes exhibitions. He has exhibited at the Panter and Hall Gallery, London, Tracey McNee Fine Art, Glasgow, Modern Artists Gallery, Reading and the Plus One Gallery, London amongst others. His paintings are held in many private and corporate collections, and he is represented in the permanent collection of the Contemporary Art Society of Wales.

www.ingramcontent.com/pod-product-compliance
Lightning Source LLC
Chambersburg PA
CBHW050855180526
45159CB00007B/2680